CULTURE
in China

Melanie Guile

Raintree

Chicago, Illinois

© 2004 Raintree
Published by Raintree, a division of Reed Elsevier, Inc.
Chicago, Illinois
Customer Service 888-363-4266
Visit our website at www.raintreelibrary.com

For information, address the publisher:
Raintree, 100 N. LaSalle, Suite 1200, Chicago, IL 60602

Printed in China by Wing King Tong.
07 06 05 04 03
10 9 8 7 6 5 4 3 2 1

Library of Congress Cataloging-in-Publication Data
Guile, Melanie.
  China / Melanie Guile.
    p. cm. -- (Culture in--)
Includes bibliographical references and index.
Contents: Culture in China -- Performing arts -- Traditions and customs
-- Costume and clothing -- Food -- Film and television -- Literature --
Women and girls -- Arts and crafts.
  ISBN 1-4109-0468-7 (library binding)
  1. China--Civilization--1976---Juvenile literature. [1.
China--Civilization--1976-] I. Title.   II. Series: Guile, Melanie.
Culture in-- .
  DS779.23.G845 2004
  951--dc21

                                    2003007045

Acknowledgments
The publisher would like to thank the following for permission to reproduce photographs:
pp. 4, 12 PhotoDisc; pp. 7 (top), 11, 13 © Wolfgang Koehler/Australian Picture Library (APL)/Corbis; p. 8 © Liu Liqun/Australian Picture Library (APL)/Corbis; pp. 9, 16, 20 Courtesy of the Hong Kong Tourism Board;
p. 10 © Tom Nebbia/Australian Picture Library (APL)/Corbis; p. 14 © Wally McNamee/Australian Picture Library (APL)/Corbis; p. 15 (top) © Keren Su/Australian Picture Library (APL)/Corbis; p. 15 (bottom)
© Langevin Jacques/Australian Picture Library (APL)/Corbis; p. 17 (top) © Dean Conger/Australian Picture Library (APL)/Corbis; p. 17 (bottom) Australian Picture Library (APL)/Corbis/© Bohemian Nomad Picturemakers; p. 18 Frederic J. Brown/AFP/AAP; p. 19 © Earl & Nazima Kowall/Australian Picture Library (APL)/Corbis; p. 21 © Bojan Brecelj/Australian Picture Library (APL)/Corbis; p. 23 (left) Michel Lipchitz/
© 2000 AP/AAP; p. 23 (right) Australian Picture Library (APL)/Corbis/© AFP; p. 24 Michel Euler/© 1999 AP/AAP; p. 25 Austral International Picture Library; p. 26 Australian Picture Library (APL)/Corbis/
© Bettmann; p. 28 Dragon Bride by Jiang Tiefeng: 33.25" x 33.25" serigraph on canvas. Published and copyrighted by Fingerhut Group Publisher, Inc., © 1998; p. 29 © Royal Ontario Museum/Australian Picture Library (APL)/Corbis.

Other Acknowledgments
Cover photograph: © Liu Luqun/Australian Picture Library/Corbis. Actors perform Peking opera in Beijing, China.

CONTENTS

Some words are shown in bold, **like this.** You can find out what they mean by looking in the glossary.

CULTURE IN CHINA

The Middle Kingdom

China is a huge country that sprawls across the world map from Europe to the Pacific Ocean. With 1.27 billion people (one-fifth of the world's population) and a culture that goes back 5,000 years, the Chinese are immensely proud of their ancient nation. It is no wonder that they have always seen themselves as the center of things, as suggested by the the Chinese word for their country, *Zhongguo,* meaning "the Middle Kingdom."

What is culture?

Culture is a people's way of living. It is the way a group of people identifies itself as separate and different from any other. Culture includes a group's spoken and written language, social customs, and habits as well as its traditions of art, craft, dance, drama, music, literature, and religion.

In the centuries after the first **dynasties** (ruling families) emerged around 2200 B.C.E., China developed sophisticated scientific knowledge much earlier than many other parts of the world. The Chinese built fine cities, canal

systems, and the 3,750-foot- (6,035-km-) long Great Wall. They invented the world's first writing, paper, and printing. They knew the Earth was round by 139 C.E. and used compasses to explore as far as India and Europe. Three of the world's most influential religions—**Taoism, Confucianism,** and **Buddhism**—emphasized the importance of obedience, harmony, self-discipline, and loyalty to family and country. All this provided a firm foundation on which a variety of arts flourished.

Chairman Mao Zedong, founder of the People's Republic of China, led the country for 27 years. Mao died in 1976 and his preserved body lies in Beijing.

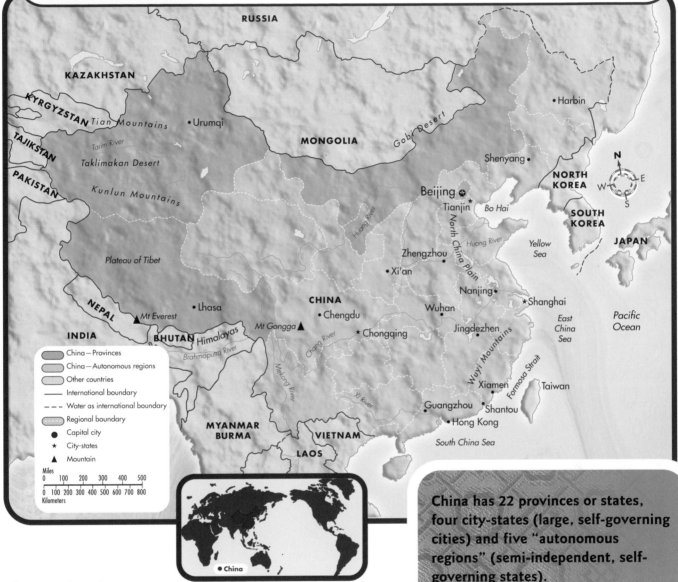

National flag of the People's Republic of China

The red background stands for the spirit of the Communist revolution. The small stars represent the four classes of people—workers, peasants, the middle classes, and the rich—who were united and made equal by the Communist Party, symbolized by the large star.

China has 22 provinces or states, four city-states (large, self-governing cities) and five "autonomous regions" (semi-independent, self-governing states).

Revolution

However, stability did not last forever. By 1900 war, famine, and **corruption** led to a great upheaval. In 1911 the powerful leader Sun Yat-sen (1867–1925) swept away the old emperors and established a **republic.** After many more years of civil war, the **Communist** Party under Mao Zedong (1893–1976) took power in the great **revolution** of 1949. The People's Republic of China was established as a communist nation, order was restored, and the lives of poor peasant farmers and workers improved. Turmoil resumed with the launch of the **Cultural Revolution** (1966–1976), Chairman Mao's movement to destroy anything remotely foreign or connected to China's non-communist past. Monasteries, temples, and galleries were burned; artists, writers, musicians, and other performers were killed or thrown out of the country.

After the Cultural Revolution

When it ended in 1976, the **Cultural Revolution** had wiped out centuries of cultural achievements in China. Since then, however, the traditional arts have undergone a revival. Peking opera, classical Chinese music, puppetry, and folk dance are supported by the government. **Martial arts,** gymnastics, and diving are sports at which the Chinese once again excel in international competitions. Chinese television series, movies, and a thriving pop music scene provide entertainment. All of this is fueled by an ongoing boom in China's economy. In recent years, the Chinese government has taken steps to loosen its rules against private ownership of property and businesses. Free enterprise has helped the economy to grow. Because of this growth, incomes have quadrupled since 1978 and the number of people living in poverty has decreased from more than 30 percent in 1978 to less than 10 percent in 1996.

A hard way of life

But the new China is still a poor, crowded country where people must work very hard to make ends meet. Basic health care, housing, and education are supplied by the government, but wealth is no longer equally shared. Thirty percent of the population lives in the cities, where people earn more than twice as much as country people. Young professionals stroll around Shanghai in designer clothes, surf the Internet, and dance to punk rock. But in the country, peasants might still plow rice fields with buffalo and live in rustic houses.

Unemployment is rising as inefficient government-run factories close, unable to compete with more profitable private ones. **AIDS** is a serious health crisis, with some experts estimating that one in four people is infected with HIV (the virus that causes AIDS) in parts of north-central China. The nation also faces an enormous pollution problem. Fifty years of uncontrolled pollution by heavy industry has taken a terrible toll on the environment. Although antipollution laws are now in place, nine of the ten most polluted cities in the world are in China. The government still practices **censorship** and exercises control over many aspects of society, and people are not free to voice negative opinions about the government.

Caught in the net

The more than 50 million Chinese who surf the Internet were astonished in 2002 when the search engines AltaVista and Google were shut down by the government, in an attempt to stop information from coming into the country. Chinese officials continue to monitor the Internet for antigovernment material.

Yin and *yang*—the search for balance

Modern life in China is busy and stressful, and many Chinese turn to ancient traditions to restore a sense of peace and harmony. Many Chinese believe that everything in the universe can be explained as a balance between *yang* (energy, light, maleness) and *yin* (stillness, darkness, femaleness). The quest to achieve this balance can be seen in numerous aspects of Chinese culture.

Every morning, people exercise with the slow movements of *tai chi* to prepare their bodies and spirits for the day ahead. Meals are prepared with a careful balance of "heating" and "cooling" foods. Chinese doctors often treat illnesses with a combination of herbal remedies, **acupuncture,** and western-style drugs. Experts in *feng shui,* an ancient method of arranging living spaces, are consulted to ensure that the design of buildings and rooms will bring luck, health, and tranquillity to the people inside them.

Ethnic groups

Another kind of harmony is particularly needed among China's 55 officially recognized **ethnic groups.** Ninety-four percent of the population is **Han Chinese,** and their native language, Mandarin, is the official language of China. Even so, seventy million people are **minorities.** Many of them have little in common with the Han. For instance, the Chinese invaded Tibet in 1950 and Tibetans have struggled to preserve their culture and traditions ever since. The Mongolians in the far northwest once formed a mighty empire that conquered the Han. The Uygurs of Xinjiang, also in the northwest, are not Asian at all, but **Caucasian Muslims.** At times China resorts to military force in order to keep its diverse peoples all part of one country.

ETHNIC MINORITIES

China has an astonishing diversity of **ethnic groups**, mostly in border regions. There are 55 officially recognized ethnic **minorities** that include about 70 million people. The Uygurs of Central Asia regard themselves as Turkish, not Asian, and would like to be independent from China. Tibet, in the far west, is a conquered country, and its people generally are not happy with being ruled by the Chinese. The government now encourages minorities to keep their distinctive cultures after long years of trying to **suppress** them.

A Kazakh family having a meal in their *yurt*.

The far-flung tribespeople

Historically the Kazakhs roamed the vast plains of central Asia on horseback with herds of sheep, goats, and cattle. Today, one million Kazakhs live in the northwestern province of Xinjiang. Some are farmers but many still live in felt tents *(yurts),* speak their own language, and write in Arabic. Kazakhs are **Muslims** and are wary of the many non-Muslim **Han Chinese** who have migrated to the Xinjiang region in recent years.

Over seven million Uygurs also live in Xinjiang. The Uygurs have much in common with the Turks, to whom they are related. They eat lamb kebab and bake wheat flat bread, follow **Islam,** and have their own folktales. They also have a unique form of opera called the *12 Mukams,* consisting of 340 songs and folk dances accompanied by strings and tambourines. More popular, however, are the locally produced Uygur-language television action shows.

Southern peoples

The southern provinces of Yunnan, Guizhou, and Guangxi hold more than half of China's ethnic groups. Two such groups are the Miao and the Jinuo. While all of these groups tend to keep up their own traditions, most members speak and write Mandarin Chinese.

The Miao

The Miao are famous for the beauty and skill of their weaving, fabric dyeing, and embroidery. An ancient Miao folktale explains their brightly colored clothing. The story tells of a young hunter who brought a pheasant home to his mother. Impressed by the color and beauty of the bird, she made a costume to match it. The bird's crest became the tall headdress, the wings became richly embroidered sleeves, the tail became the short, pleated skirt and belt, and the legs became colored leg-wrappings.

The Jinuo

The 18,000 Jinuo living in the mountains of Yunnan were officially recognized as a minority group relatively recently, in 1979. They have no written language, but speak a language called Youle. Traditionally, up to twenty families shared large huts with thatched roofs raised on stilts.

The Jinuo worship nature and the Sun, and pay tribute to harvest spirits in their famous Big Drum Dance *(Echeguo)*. They are known for their stretched earlobes plugged with thick bamboo sticks (or flowers, for couples in love). Women wear white hoods and black tunics with striking red and white stripes. Though it is now less common, women used to blacken their teeth with pear-tree sap.

This Jinuo girl is wearing a traditional costume.

Ox Soul Festival

Oxen are the working animals of the Zhuang people of Guangxi in the far south, but not at Ox Soul Festival. On this Birthday of the Ox King, all oxen are rested and fed on steamed black rice to ensure a good harvest. The Zhuang are the **indigenous** people of Guangxi and they have a rich culture of song and dance.

WOMEN AND GIRLS

Confucianism teaches that women and girls should be obedient to husbands and fathers. Although women were respected as homemakers, it was very rare for a woman to receive an education or work in a paid job. From ancient times until the 1911 **revolution** of Sun Yat-sen, girls of the wealthy classes had their feet broken and tightly bound with bandages to keep them from growing, since tiny feet were considered more attractive.

Equal opportunity

The Chinese **communists** were committed to equal treatment of men and women. They banned foot binding and made elementary education a requirement for both girls and boys. The Marriage Law of 1950 ended the total control men had previously had over their wives, and required goods to be distributed equally to divorcing couples. Women were expected to do paid work and many were assigned high-level jobs.

Women and girls today

Although under the communists the most powerful jobs were still in men's hands, women experienced improvement in their economic positions. However, now that the government plays less of a role in what businesses do, women in China are finding themselves less well off. Women's salaries are 23 percent less than men's, and they are also twice as likely to be unemployed.

Although nine years of

The communists improved the lot of women by making schooling compulsory for girls.

school are required, many country girls (particularly among **ethnic groups**) are kept home to help on the farms. While 82 percent of males can read and write, only 62 percent of females can, and only 25 percent of university students are women. Everywhere in China fathers still are the family leaders and make most decisions, although wives do have a strong influence in household matters.

One Child Policy

Mao's successor, Deng Xiaoping, launched a program in 1979 to slow the country's rapid population growth. Called the One Child Policy, it made having more than one child illegal. Benefits for one-child families include cash, better health care, and free education. Illegal births are punished with large fines. In recent years the policy has been softened and most peasants are now allowed two children, especially if the first child is a girl.

Boys are valued as breadwinners for poor peasant families, so couples try to make sure their one child is a boy. People have been known to neglect, abandon, or even kill baby girls. Along with these serious problems, too many baby boys are being born —an average of 117 boys to 100 girls (the normal ratio is 106 to 100). Wives are becoming scarce, and in rural areas young women are sometimes kidnapped and married by force. Government crackdowns on wife stealing have not yet been very effective.

This Shanghai billboard promotes China's One Child Policy.

Hard labor

Many extremely poor peasant girls move to the big cities like Beijing and Shanghai seeking work. City factories are packed with such girls working twelve to sixteen hours per day in terrible conditions for very poor wages. Unfortunately, many end up homeless. Modern slave traders often target rural women, promising them great jobs in the city. Instead of being delivered to their new "jobs," they are sold and forced to work without pay.

Little emperors

Under the One Child Policy, many families now have only sons. These children are often known as "little emperors" because they are so spoiled by their parents. Many are overweight from eating too many treats, and ambitious parents are going to extremes to get their sons into the best schools. The One Child Policy has been criticized around the world, but it has been very successful in slowing China's population growth to just under two children per family.

13

COSTUME
and Clothing

The Chinese have been known for their fine wardrobes since 2640 B.C.E. when Empress Hsi Ling Shi first wove fabric from the thread of the silkworm. **Ethnic groups** in China's southeast are also famous for their distinctive, handmade costumes.

Traditional dress

Boys wearing Mao suits and caps.

The *qipao*, a fitted women's dress made of silk with a high collar and slit skirt, is regarded as the Chinese national costume for women. It was traditionally worn with trousers, but in the early 1900s women wore it short with silk stockings as a daring fashion statement. After the **communist** revolution in 1949, the government banned traditional clothing and replaced it with a loose-fitting outfit for both men and women known as a "Mao suit," which was worn with a cap.

Since the 1970s when the Chinese government relaxed some of its policies, western fashions have become popular. Jeans and business suits are especially common in the cities. International fashion shows are staged every year in Shanghai and Beijing to promote young designers. Some peasants, however, still wear traditional cone-shaped hats and plain, loose jackets and pants.

Everything old is new again

Traditional Chinese clothes are the latest fashion craze in Beijing and Shanghai. Popular items include embroidered silk jackets with braided buttons and the women's *qipao*. The *qipao* dress was rediscovered when the movie star Gong Li took to wearing them. Now every city boutique has racks of *qipao* in exciting new colors and fabrics. The traditional *dudo* is a tight-fitting top with a halter neck tied at the back by strings. For thousands of years it was worn as underwear, but now it is worn with jeans by the young and trendy.

Color coding

The colors people choose to wear in China have important meanings. Blue, for instance, stands for power, and red means happiness and luck. Traditionally the *dudo* (Chinese underwear) was made of red silk because it was considered lucky to wear red against the skin.

14

On special occasions Miao women wear striking headdresses. They make a special wig out of linen, wool, and the hair of their ancestors. The wig is then wrapped around a headpiece made of water buffalo horns.

Tribal costumes

The ethnic groups in China's southeastern provinces are renowned for the beauty of their handmade costumes. The Miao wear clothing made of black cloth that is richly embroidered with striking red, blue, and white designs. Visitors are always impressed by their full, pleated skirts, embroidered aprons, and hats shaped like animal horns. The Ge are famous for their *batik* fabrics, made by painting designs in wax and then dyeing the cloth a deep blue. The Dong of Guizhou are also known for their skillful embroidery. It is said that the brightly decorated skullcaps worn by Dong babies ward off evil spirits, who mistake the infants for flowers and pass them by.

This dress by fashion designer Wu Haiyan was inspired by the bright colors worn by tribespeople in southeast China. In 1997 Haiyan was named one of China's top ten designers. Her designs have also been successful abroad.

Yi wedding customs

The Yi people of Yunnan make a special wedding costume, which the bride keeps for the rest of her life. The bride-to-be sews a pair of pants for the groom, but she stitches the leg openings shut. At the wedding celebration, the groom has to get the trousers on as quickly as he can. He then wears them every day until his first child is born. Then they are used as a wrap for the baby.

15

FOOD

The ancient Chinese wise man Confucius said, "Eating is the first happiness," and eating together is an important part of family life in China. Most meals include rice except in the north, where wheat is grown and used to make breads, dumplings, and wheat noodles. Protein-rich soybean curd (tofu) is eaten throughout China. The Chinese invented tea and they drink it with every meal, without milk or sugar. There are four main styles of food in China, named after the regions where they were developed: Cantonese, Eastern, Northern, and Sichuan.

Cantonese

Cantonese food is known throughout the world. The fertile southern coast of Guangdong (the region around Guangzhou) supplies seafood, fresh vegetables, and an amazing variety of meats (chicken, snake, monkey, and even dog). Freshness and invention are important in Cantonese cooking. Food is usually chopped and steamed or stir-fried very quickly in lightly flavored sauces. Rice is served with every meal.

The Cantonese invented *dim sum*. This is a style of cuisine in which morsels of delicious food are cooked in bamboo baskets and wheeled around the restaurant on trolleys. Diners choose dozens of different dishes for their meal. Chicken feet, shrimp dumplings, and steamed pork buns are very popular.

In a restaurant *dim sum* specialties like these would be served from carts. *Dim sum* means "to touch the heart" in Chinese.

Eastern style

Near the eastern cities of Shanghai and Suzhou, the mouth of the fertile Chang (Yangtze) River and coastal fishing grounds provide abundant ingredients. Clams, carp, pork, and chicken are stir-fried and served in delicious sauces. Fresh vegetables and rice provide an important contrast to the fattier meats such as eel and duck.

> Preparing Peking duck is an art form in northern China. After the ducks are killed and plucked, they are glazed and the bodies are filled with boiling water. Next they are roasted over an open fire, and then the water is drained out to make duck soup.

Northern regions

Rice will not grow in the cold north, so wheat and another edible grain called millet are used to make dumplings and noodles. The northern peoples, the Manchus and Mongols, were once **nomadic** horsemen who cooked their food over campfires, so their traditional foods are roasted meats (especially lamb) and hot stews.

Northern dishes tend to be more starchy and fatty than other Chinese styles of cooking, because people need hearty foods for energy during the icy winters. Steamed pigeon with yams, stir-fried jellyfish, and Peking duck (roasted duck with crispy skin) are all good examples of northern cuisine.

Sichuan style

Sichuan food, from the south-central region around Chengdu, has become famous around the world for its hot and spicy flavors. Red chilies and other fiery spices like garlic, pepper, and ginger are stir-fried with pork and chicken, which are often soaked in flavored liquids or pickled before cooking.

Cup of tea, anyone?

Around 2700 B.C.E. the Chinese discovered that the dried leaves of a native camellia bush (*Camellia sinensis*) made a good drink when steeped in boiling water. From China the drink spread first to India and Sri Lanka (where most of the world's tea is grown today) and then to Europe in the 1700s. Some research has shown that drinking tea can have important health benefits.

Music

The **communist** government in China strongly supports traditional music, which is taught and performed in academies all over the country. Western classical music is also popular in the cities, and many of the world's great classical performers have come from China. Pop, rock, and punk music are popular, too, particularly in Hong Kong.

Traditional

Chinese music is based on a five-tone scale (unlike the eight-tone scale used in Western music) and it sounds very different from classical music composed by Europeans. A traditional Chinese orchestra has four sections: bowed strings, plucked strings, flutes, and percussion (mostly gongs and drums). The plucked strings include zithers, such as the ancient seven-stringed *guqin,* which noblemen were once required to learn.

Pop and rock

Young, female solo artists or clean-cut boy bands singing sweet, romantic songs are all the rage in Chinese pop music. Andy Lau is a pop singer and actor from Hong Kong who has become a superstar all over China. Fei Wang, a female singer, was briefly married to another pop star, Dou Wei, who is notorious for having lip-synched (moved his lips to his own recorded music) at concerts.

Mountaintop music

China's first outdoor rock festival was held in 2000. The Snow Mountain Festival was organized by rock legend Cui Jian (pictured above), and it attracted 10,000 fans. Held in Lijiang, a southern town over 12,000 feet (3,700 meters) above sea level, the concert was billed as the highest-altitude rock festival ever. Performers had to take breaths of oxygen on stage between songs.

Cui Jian brought rock music to China when he amazed the crowd at a 1986 concert with a song called "Nothing to my Name." The song became an anthem for student **democracy** rallies in the 1980s, and Cui performed in Tiananmen Square just fifteen days before the massacre in 1989.

Punk rock, hip-hop, and every other type of modern music can be heard in Beijing's dance clubs, but always under the watchful eye of the authorities who might stop music from being played if it seems antigovernment.

A Chinese acrobat balances on her mouth while spinning cloth circles with her hands and feet.

Movement and dance

Acrobatics

Acrobatics have been performed in China since about 500 B.C. and grew out of ancient folk dance and **martial arts** traditions. Common acrobatic skills include tightrope walking, juggling, balancing, diving through hoops, and performing magic tricks. In the famous Lion Dance, dancers imitate lions by jumping and rolling around holding large, decorated lion heads. "Meteor juggling" involves swinging glass bowls filled with water around on ropes without spilling a drop. Chinese acrobats are spectacular athletes, and begin their training early in childhood.

Dance

The 55 **ethnic groups** in China all have their own folk dances. Generally they are based on ancient tales, and are performed outdoors for festivals and holy days. In the folk dances of the **Han Chinese,** elaborate costumes are worn and dancers hold props such as fans, flags, and batons. Movements can be graceful or athletic and energetic.

China's first modern dance school was Guangdong Modern Dance Company in Guangzhou. It was set up by Yang Mei-qi in 1987, and blends ballet, folk, and modern dance styles borrowed from the United States. Now modern dance is also taught in the famous school for classical ballet, the Beijing Dance Academy.

On the stage

Chinese opera

Chinese opera began about 800 years ago, during the Yuan Dynasty (1279–1368). It combines acting, singing, dance, music, **martial arts,** and lavish costumes. Accompanied by a traditional Chinese orchestra, actors play heroes and villains in heroic or tragic stories. The performance is not meant to be natural and realistic; movements are formal, and masklike makeup clearly expresses each character's personality. Traditionally men played all the female parts and women were not allowed to perform. Today female opera stars are common and many of them play men's parts!

A Peking opera performer applies the traditional masklike makeup.

More than 300 different forms of opera exist, but the most famous is Peking opera, which originated in Beijing when the city was known as Peking (its name was officially changed to Beijing in 1979). Mei Lanfang (1894–1961) is regarded as the country's greatest performer. He brought Chinese opera to the United States, Japan, and Russia, and his skill at playing female roles was legendary.

Modern drama

Western-style theater existed during the 1920s and 1930s in China, but war interrupted its development. In 1952 the Beijing People's Art Theater was set up by actor and playwright Cao Yu (1910–1996). Regarded as the founder of modern Chinese drama, he wrote many classic plays that are still performed today. Lao She (1899–1966) is the country's best-loved playwright. His work, *Teahouse* (1957), about historical and social change over three generations, may be China's most famous play. Lao She died tragically when his works were called into question by authorities during the **Cultural Revolution.**

PERFORMING ARTS

20

Puppetry

Puppetry goes back 2,000 years in China, and there are three different forms. Rod puppets are worked from below using thin metal rods. Shadow puppets, made of leather cutouts, are lit from behind so that their shadows are cast on a screen. String puppets (marionettes) are worked from above by a puppeteer who can be seen by the audience. Marionettes are made of carved wood and have up to 30 strings. In the hands of a master, they can seem extremely lifelike. Marionette puppetry has its own music called "puppet tunes." Quanzhou Puppet Theatre, run for 50 years by a great puppet master named Huang Yi Que, is the premiere marionette troupe in China.

These are rod puppets owned by a Shanghai puppet theater.

No Man's Land Theater Company

Hong Kong is a thriving center for modern theater. Tang Shu-wing is famous around the world as an actor and director. In 1997 he established a company, No Man's Land, that produces works incorporating traditional and modern forms of puppetry, video, and other forms of multimedia. In 2002 Tang directed the Nobel Prize-winning author Gao Xingjian's play, *Between Life and Death* (1991).

LITERATURE

Words of the ancients

Poems and stories have been written in China since around 1000 B.C.E., when song lyrics by an unknown author were collected into a book called the *Shijing*. Another collection, the *Songs of Chu,* was composed in about 200 B.C.E. These works became the great classics of Chinese poetry.

Classical poets

China's most famous poet is Li Bai (701–762 C.E.), also known as Li Po, who lived during the Tang Dynasty (618–907), a golden age of art and literature. He grew up in Sichuan in southern China and traveled all over the country, writing about the beauty of nature, the joy of friendship, and the sorrow of parting. About 2,000 of Li Bai's poems survive. His poetry is still very popular and continues to be studied in schools.

Du Fu (712–770) was a friend of Li Bai. Du Fu is especially famous for his poems that criticize war, bloodshed of any kind, and poverty. At the age of 47, Du Fu built himself a thatched hut in the town of Chengdu and wrote 240 poems there. There is now a garden and museum on the site.

Stories from the past

Novels appeared in China in the late 1300s and became very popular. They were written in a mix of the classical script used only by scholars and the everyday written language used by common people. *The Water Margin* (also known as *Rebels of the Marsh*), written in the 1300s, is a famous novel set in the Song Dynasty (960–1279) about a group of adventurers. *Journey to the West* (or *Monkey Magic*) by Wu Cheng'en (written about 1570) is a book based on the life of a **Buddhist** monk named Xuan Zang who travels to India. Animal and spirit companions travel with him and their antics make the story very lively. The well-known novel *Dream of Red Mansions,* written around 1760 by Cao Xueqin, is about a large, wealthy family in Beijing.

Nobel Prize winner

In 2000 the writer Gao Xingjian (born 1940) won the Nobel Prize for Literature. His works, such as *Soul Mountain* (1999) and *One Man's Bible* (1999) cannot be sold in China because they criticize the policies of the **communist** government. Gao Xingjian fled his homeland in 1987 and is now a French citizen. He is pictured at left.

Modern literature

Until about 1900 most literature in China was written in an ancient language called *wenyan* or *guwen*, which only scholars could understand. But in the early 1900s, writers began to produce works that were written entirely in everyday script. Lu Xun (1881–1936) is considered the father of modern Chinese literature. He wrote dark, moody short stories on modern themes like "Diary of a Madman" (1918) and "The Story of Ah Q." (1921–1922). Lao She (1899–1966) wrote about the desperate poverty of Beijing street life in *Rickshaw Boy* (1936).

Punk Lit

Over 10 million copies of Wang Shuo's books are in print in China, and he even writes for Hollywood. A movie he wrote called *Baba* received a "Best Film" award at a film festival in Switzerland.

Under Chairman Mao writing was strictly controlled, but today's writers are becoming bolder and challenging **censorship.** Wang Shuo (born 1958) is the best known of the new young writers called the Punk Lit Group. He has written more than twenty novels, as well as film and television scripts, most dealing with controversial topics. His works were condemned as "spiritual pollution" by the government and some were even banned, but nevertheless Wang Shuo has a huge following in China.

FILM
and Television

Silver screen

Chinese films were made during the 1930s and 1940s, mostly in Shanghai, exploring the difficulties of life in war-torn China. Director Fei Mu (1906–1951) made the great classic *Spring in a Small Town* (1948), which has been called the best Chinese film of all time. After 1949 the **communists** used film as **propaganda**, and all filmmaking that did not promote communism was banned during the **Cultural Revolution** (1966–1976).

Chen Huaikai was a famous filmmaker under Mao, but in 1966 during the Cultural Revolution, he was forced to stop working when his 14-year-old son publicly denounced him and handed him over to the **Red Guards.** That son, Chen Kaige, deeply regretted his action, and eventually became a filmmaker himself. Today Chen Kaige is one of China's most famous directors. He won first prize at Cannes Film Festival for *Farewell My Concubine* in 1993.

Chen Kaige's friend, the director Zhang Yimou (born 1950), is admired around the world for his sensitive, visually stunning films, including *Red Sorghum* (1988) and *Raise the Red Lantern* (1991). Both films made their leading actress Gong Li (born 1965) an international star. Many of Zhang's films are banned in China. Tian Zhuangzhuang is another filmmaker who is regarded as dangerous by the government. A film set in Tibet titled *The Horse Thief* (1986) and his famous study of the Cultural Revolution, *The Blue Kite*, (1993) are both banned.

Madame Mao

Jiang Qing (ca. 1914–1991) started out as a Shanghai movie actress in the 1930s and 1940s. She was later known as Madame Mao, Mao Zedong's extremely influential wife. In 1980 she was put on trial for contributing to the horrors that occurred during the Cultural Revolution. She denied the charges, but was found guilty and spent the rest of her life in prison.

Actress Gong Li (left) and director Chen Kaige.

24

This scene is from director Chen Kaige's film *The Emperor and the Assassin* (1999), the most expensive Chinese film ever made.

Kung fu movies

Known as kung fu action movies in the West, Hong Kong films are popular throughout Asia. These adventure movies featuring superheroes with magical powers are called *Wu Xia* films in Hong Kong. Jackie Chan is the best-known maker of these films. John Woo's kung fun-style movie *A Better Tomorrow* was copied by many directors in the 1980s.

Small screen

The majority of houses in China have a television. Most programs are produced by the government-run Chinese Central Television (CCTV) and content is strictly controlled. Programs include news, dramas, crime shows, documentaries, and light entertainment, but the most popular are soap operas made in local studios. Chinese television includes advertisements and foreign programs, although these are often **censored.** It was reported that former leader Deng Xiaoping's favorite program was the U.S. soap opera *Dynasty*. A foreign company called Star TV brought cable programs to mainland China in 2001.

ARTS AND CRAFTS

Over thousands of years in China, styles of painting, calligraphy, pottery, and carving changed very little. Artists strove to perfect the techniques handed down from ancient masters. Self-expression was not as important as faithfully following tradition and creating works of beauty and spiritual harmony. With the end of the Qing **Dynasty** in 1911, modern art was born. However, after the **revolution** in 1949, all artists were directed to produce works for the government, mostly portraits of Chairman Mao and happily smiling peasants and workers. Since government reforms starting in the mid-1970s, however, a thriving new art scene has emerged.

Traditional painting

Peace and harmony between man and nature are basic to **Taoism,** and these elements are vital in traditional Chinese art. Simple lines on plain backgrounds are common and color is used sparingly. Ink and brushes are used on the finest paper (called *xuan*) or on silk. Flowing brushwork is very important in Chinese art. Landscapes, portraits, and detailed studies of nature (called the Bird and Flower style) capture the beauty of a fleeting moment. Most traditional paintings include calligraphy (often a poem) and the artist's seal or stamp.

This painting in the Bird and Flower style is called *The Five-Colored Parakeet,* by Emperor Hui-tsung (early 1100s C.E.).

Many **ethnic groups** in China are famous for the beauty of their handicrafts. The Jili women of the southern island province of Hainan use ancient "backstrap" looms to weave intricately patterned cloth. Made of two bamboo poles, the loom has a strap that runs around the woman's waist as she sits on the ground. She adjusts the tightness of the warp threads by leaning forward or back.

A Chinese artist works at his calligraphy, which is a highly regarded art form in China.

Old masters

The first great Chinese artist was Ku K'ai-chi, who lived around 344–406. He was a master of human figure painting, although he also painted landscapes. Only three copies of his works survive. His scroll titled *Admonitions of the Instructress to the Court Ladies* is one of the oldest known Chinese paintings.

Wang Wei (699–759) was a famous poet and musician as well as a painter, and he became an artist at the emperor's court. His landscapes painted in black ink are admired for their misty, magical atmosphere. Experts are not sure whether any of Wang Wei's paintings survive, although the famous *Villa on Zhonguan Mountain* is often attributed to him.

Pan Tianshou (1897–1971) was known throughout the world. He was the first to create huge, bold landscapes using traditional "splashed ink" techniques and bold brushwork. His beautiful paintings of birds, insects, and flowers are in galleries around the world and have even appeared on postage stamps.

Calligraphy

Each character in Chinese writing is a kind of word picture, so it is not surprising that the skill of writing (calligraphy) is an art form in China. The "four treasures" of the study of calligraphy are paper, the ink stick, the ink stone (for mixing the powdered ink), and brushes. The same tools are used for traditional Chinese painting. Many different styles of script exist, but all emphasize the flow, grace, and flair of the brush strokes. Calligraphy is still a highly regarded skill and is used today on banners, flags, important documents and paintings, and in temples.

Modern art

Artists in China have had a difficult time since the **communist** revolution in 1949. Chairman Mao enforced strict rules about the kinds of art people could create, so self-expression was impossible. During the **Cultural Revolution** (1966–1976) things got much worse. Most artists were forced to stop working and were sent to country work-camps for "re-education." Many were beaten and even murdered. The government reforms of the late 1970s have led to a rebirth of art in China, although the government still uses its power to control it.

Today's masters

Han Meilin (born 1937) is one of China's most famous artists. A sculptor, painter, graphic designer, and calligrapher who lives in Beijing, Han blends western and Chinese folk art traditions in his work, and is well known in China as the designer of the red phoenix logo for the airline, Air China. He also designed the Five Dragon Clock Tower in Atlanta for the 1996 Olympic Games, and his paintings have appeared on **United Nations** Christmas cards. Han's massive 5,291-ton (4,800–metric ton), 138-foot (42-meter) –long granite sculpture *Group Tigers* attracts many tourists in Dalian, in northeast China.

The painting *Dragon Bride* (1998), by Jiang Tiefeng, is a serigraph—a silkscreen print.

Fang Fengfu (born 1937) works as a professor, artist, and calligrapher in Hong Kong and has been awarded several international art prizes. He uses rich, bright colors to paint traditional designs of flowers, birds, and trees, as in his famous *Brilliant Autumn Scenery* (ca. 1993).

Jiang Tiefeng (born 1938) made a living under the communists by painting **propaganda** posters (including a famous poster of Chairman Mao).

Jiang is China's best-known illustrator of children's books (including the award-winning *Two Little Peacocks*, published in 1974). His oil paintings are also very well known. In 1979 he painted a mural called *Stone Forest* in the Great Hall of the People in Beijing. Painted on six silk panels, the mural took seven months to complete. He now lives in the United States.

Porcelain

A delicate pottery called porcelain was invented by the Chinese around 200 C.E. It was exported to Europe for over 1,000 years before the secret of how to make it leaked out. The town of Jingdezhen in Jiangxi Province has always been the main source of kaolin, the famous white clay that is porcelain's main ingredient. Today, Jingdezhen has dozens of factories, a porcelain research institute, and a museum. Many of China's master potters are also based here. They make reproductions of traditional designs, including the blue and white Ming **Dynasty** (1368-1644) style and the handpainted scenes of the Qing Dynasty (1644–1912).

Making an impression

Artist Dai Guangyu is making an impact with performance art, a type of art that focuses more on the process of making it than on the finished product. In his work *Making Traces* (1997), the artist lies down in a grave lined with paper in a Shuangliu cemetery. The mixture of mud and sweat leaves a print of the artist's body on the paper. Another artwork involves taking apples from a fruit vendor, painting them gold, then returning them to the vendor and paying for them.

The Chinese closely guarded the secret of how to make their highly prized porcelain, such as these vases from the Ming and Qing Dynasties, for hundreds of years.

GLOSSARY

acupuncture traditional Chinese medical practice involving the insertion of needles into the skin

AIDS (Acquired Immune Deficiency Syndrome) often fatal disease caused by HIV (human immunodeficiency virus), which is transmitted through contact with blood or bodily fluids of an infected person

ancestor person from whom one is descended

Buddhism religion founded by the Buddha, also known as Gautama Buddha (563 B.C.E.–483 B.C.E.). Followers of Buddhism (known as Buddhists) study the teachings of the Buddha and strive for a peaceful state called enlightenment.

Caucasian any of the race of people known as white, specifically those of Europe, southwest Asia, and northern Africa

censored having had something removed because it was considered inappropriate for people to see, read, or hear

censorship practice of preventing certain ideas or information from being freely communicated to the public

Christianity religion based on the belief in one god and the teachings of Jesus, as written in a holy book called the Bible. A follower of Christianity is a Christian.

communist belonging to a communist political party or having a government based on the ideas of communism. In communism the government controls all property and industry, and provides each citizen with food, housing, and jobs.

Confucianism religion based on the ideas of the ancient Chinese wise man, Confucius (ca. 551–479 B.C.E.)

corruption dishonest or criminal behavior for personal gain, especially in reference to government officials or other powerful people

Cultural Revolution movement in China launched by Communist Party Chairman Mao, lasting from 1966 to 1977, to enforce the ideals of communism and rid the country of foreign or antigovernment influences

democracy form of government in which decisions are made by elected representatives

dynasty period in which a country has a series of rulers from the same family

ethnic group people who share a specific culture, language, and background

Han Chinese largest of China's ethnic groups, making up 94 percent of the population

indigenous original or native to a particular country or area

Islam religion of Muslims, who believe in one god, called Allah. Muslims follow the teachings of the prophet Mohammed, which are written about in a holy book called the Koran.

less-developed world general term for the poorer countries of the world, whose economies depend mainly on farming rather than industry

martial arts traditional sports in many Asian countries that are derived from ancient techniques for fighting in battle

minority group that makes up a small percentage of a region's total population

Muslim having to do with Islam or a person who follows the Islamic religion

nomadic having a lifestyle in which one roams from place to place without ever settling, usually following seasonal food supplies for flocks or herds

propaganda materials (such as posters, brochures, or movies) that promote a set of beliefs or ideas to the public

Red Guard young Chinese civilian, often a student, who acted as an unofficial soldier to enforce the principles of the Cultural Revolution (1966–1976)

republic government led by someone who is not a monarch

revolution complete change, usually by force, from one government or political system to another

suppress to put an end to activities or silence opinions that are considered unacceptable, especially to a group in power

Taoism religion founded in the 500s B.C.E. by a Chinese scholar named Laotzu, based on a philosophy called "the way"—a path toward living harmoniously with nature

FURTHER
Reading

Allan, Tony. *Rise of Modern China.* Chicago: Heinemann, 2002.

Chen, Da. *China's Son: Growing Up in the Cultural Revolution.* New York: Random House, 2003.

Higgenbottom, Trevor, and Tony White. *China.* Chicago: Heinemann, 2001.

Keeler, Stephen. *The Changing Face of China.* Chicago: Raintree, 2003.

Simonds, Nina, and others. *Moonbeams, Dumplings, and Dragon Boats: A Treasury of Chinese Holiday Tales, Activities and Recipes.* New York: Gulliver Books, 2002.

INDEX